PISTON-POWERED PROPLINERS 1958-2000

PISTON-POWERED PROPLINERS 1958-2000

MARTIN W. BOWMAN

MBI Publishing Company

Author's note

Piston-powered Propliners 1958–2000 is the first of four Airlife airliner titles, and covers the piston-engined airliners. *Timeless Turboprops* covers the same period's finest turbine-powered aircraft, while *Jetliner Generation* covers the jet airliner era. *Wide Bodies* will cover the American 'jumbos' and the wide-bodied aircraft from Europe and Russia. The majority of data and individual aircraft histories for the aircraft in all three titles have been obtained from these invaluable tomes: *Jet Airliner Production List*, *Turbo Prop Airliner Production List* and *Piston Engine Airliner Production List*, all produced by Messrs John Roach and Tony Eastwood. Copies are available from The Aviation Hobby Shop, 4 Horton Parade, Horton Road, West Drayton, Middlesex, UB7 8EA. Details of aircraft accidents have mostly been taken from *Airlife's Register of Aircraft Accidents*, compiled by Antonio Bordoni.

Acknowledgements

I would like to make special mention of the City of Norwich Aviation Museum (CONAM) and Graham M. Simons and his wife Anne, both of GMS Enterprises, who provided the foundation for this book with a wealth of transparencies. Air Britain historian Phil Kemp very kindly supplied photos, and also 'beat the bushes' to find additional material. I am also very grateful to all of the following people, each of whom loaned photos and slides, as well as their time and expertise: Paula Allen; Jerry Cullum; Graham Dinsdale of Ian Allan Travel; Tony and Janet Eastwood; Peter Garwood; David Grimer; Tony Hudson; Derek N. James; Stan Lee; Barry Reeve; Kelvin Sloper; Lyn Taylor, British World Airlines Ltd; and Walt Truax.

Martin W. Bowman
Norwich

This edition first published in 2000 by MBI Publishing Company, 729 Prospect Avenue, PO Box 1, Osceola, WI 54020-0001 USA

© 2000 Martin W. Bowman

Previously published by Airlife Publishing Ltd., Shrewsbury, England.

MBI Publishing Company books are also available at discounts in bulk quantity for industrial or sales-promotional use. For details write to Special Sales Manager at Motorbooks International Wholesalers & Distributors, 729 Prospect Avenue, PO Box 1, Osceola, WI 54020-0001 USA.

Library of Congress Cataloging-in-Publication Data Available.

ISBN 0-7603-1012-2

Printed in Singapore.

Contents

A Scottish Aviation Twin Pioneer of Australia-based Skygear International/ Capricorn Air skirts the rocky coastline of New South Wales, which juts into the beautiful Tasman Sea. It was operating a flight from Bankstown Airport on 17 October 1988.
(*Author*)

DC-3 5Y-AAE of Air Kenya was photographed at Keekorok in the Masai Mara game reserve after a flight from Wilson Airport, Nairobi, on 23 February 1993. Tourists from Keekorok Lodge Hotel prepare to board for the flight to Wilson.

Dakotas were ideal for flights to and from the Mara, although lack of facilities at airstrips could cause problems if an aircraft burst a tyre or suffered a mechanical breakdown. Scheduled services once included twice-daily flights to the Mara and a thrice-weekly service to Lamu, an old Arab trading port which has remained largely unaltered since the nineteenth century. The Dakotas also provided an ancillary service, carrying relief supplies to drought-stricken areas in northern Kenya and taking deaf Nairobi school children on half-hour pleasure flights. They also performed medevac duties, carrying sick patients from outlying areas to hospital in Nairobi.
(*Author*)

United Airlines DC-7 N6316C *Mainliner Oahu* at Baltimore, Maryland, in June 1958. N6316C was accepted by United on 23 September 1954 and was later renamed *Mainliner Hartford*. BMR Aviation Ltd was N6316C's last operator, buying the aircraft on 10 September 1963.
(*Walt Truax*)

On 1 January 1946 BOAC's BEA Division was formed to take over the services operated by RAF Transport Command from Croydon Airport, London. On 4 March BEA began operating under civil markings and was finally formed as an independent airline on 1 August, using several DC-3s on lease from BOAC. By 1956, BEA had a fleet of over fifty Pioneer Class DC-3s, such as G-AHCV (C-47A 42-92622), an ex-RAF Mk III. The fleet of DC-3s was operated until 1962. Charlie Victor was broken up at Southend in January 1970. (*CONAM*)

ABOVE: Douglas DC-3 G-ALXN *Sir Henry Royce*. In 1951 this aircraft became one of two (G-AMDB being the other) to have its Twin Wasps replaced by 1,400 shp Dart turboprops, the type used in 1952 to power the world's first turboprop airliner, the Viscount. The two Dakotas were thus the first turbine-powered aircraft to be used commercially in the world. In March 1953 both Lima November and Delta Bravo were converted back to standard Pratt & Whitney Twin Wasp-powered aircraft. (*CONAM*)

LEFT: Vickers 636 Viking G-AJJN *Vulcan*, later *Sir Charles Napier*, first flew on 6 April 1947. It was accepted by British European Airways Corporation on 13 December 1949. During eight years of operation with BEA, Vickers Vikings flew 65 million miles, carried over 2¾ million passengers and earned £35 million in revenue. Not bad for an aircraft that used the engine nacelles, undercarriage and, initially, the geodetic outer wings of the wartime Wellington bomber. When BKS Air Transport bought Juliet November on 13 December 1954, the aircraft acquired a new name, *Jim Mollinson*. G-AJJN was subsequently owned by Continental Air Services, East Anglian Flying Services and finally Channel Airways, before it was broken up in April 1964.

(*via Derek N. James*)

In 1937 ten Stratoliners were ordered by US airlines: four by Pan American Airways; five by Transcontinental and Western Air (now Trans World Airlines – TWA); and a single aircraft by Howard Hughes. The first 307, an S-307 for PAA, flew on 31 December 1938, but was lost on a subsequent test flight. In 1944 Stratoliners were returned to Boeing for reconversion to airline standards. An outstanding feature of the newly named Stratocruiser, thanks to its circular cross-section, was its

pioneering use of cabin pressurisation for passenger comfort at substratospheric altitudes. The design also permitted room for a maximum of thirty-three passengers and five crew, including, for the first time, a flight engineer. Post-war, the revamped Stratocruisers, now fitted with replacement B-17G components, could carry thirty-eight passengers.

Model 377-10-32 G-AKGH was accepted by BOAC on 16 November 1949 and was named *RMA Caledonia* on 1 July 1950. In

total, BOAC acquired seventeen Stratocruisers (four later operated with SAS). In 1958 Transocean Air Lines of Oakland, California, bought thirteen of these, including G-AKGH (now N137A), on 4 August. In 1963 N137A was withdrawn from use, put into storage at Mojave, California, and broken up.
(*via CONAM*)

Lockheed achieved success with its four-engined Model 49 airliner, which the company had begun designing in 1938. Pan Am and TWA had showed initial interest and the Model 44 Excalibur, with accommodation for 21 passengers and a top speed of 241 mph, was developed. This led, in 1939, to a bigger and faster design, the Model 49 Constellation. TWA and Pan Am each ordered 40 Double Cyclone-powered Constellations (Connies), but with the outbreak of war, production switched instead to 180 C-69 long-range transports for the USAAF. Only 15 C-69s were delivered, but these were followed by 233 civil airliner versions.

L-749A N6008C *Star of Indiana* '808' was delivered to TWA on 7 September 1950. It was withdrawn from use and stored at Kansas City in November 1966. On 16 May 1968 N6008C was bought by Aero-Tech Inc., and it was broken up in June.
(*CONAM*)

The Avro York was a wartime innovation, a new fuselage being mated with the wings, Merlin engines and undercarriage of the Lancaster. In March 1944 a few twelve-seat mixed passenger-cargo versions were placed in service by BOAC. When York production ceased in April 1948, most of the 256 examples built had been for RAF Transport Command. Many subsequently found their way onto the civil register, operating with the short-lived British South American Airways and, later, Skyways of London, Dan-Air, and Hunting-Clan in the UK.

York I LV-XGP, later LV-AFZ, was accepted by Flota Mercante Argentina (renamed Aerolineas Argentinas) in 1946. Eagle Aviation bought the aircraft, now registered G-AMGK, on 28 December 1950, and Skyways purchased it on 25 November 1952. It was used on trooping flights in the early 1950s. Golf Kilo was finally broken up at Stansted, Essex, in July 1961. (*CONAM*)

Thousands of war-surplus Douglas C-47s and C-53s were sold off by the US Government and many came into their own with emergent airlines around the globe. After the Second World War more than 200 pre-war civil DC-3s were still in operation with airlines. Cathay Pacific's DC-3 (C-47 Skytrain) VH-MAL was built at Long Beach, California, in June 1942. It served overseas until August 1943, but was declared surplus in October 1945. It was bought in 1946 upon the formation of Cathay Pacific. On 3 October 1946 Alpha Lima became VH-HDB and was named *Betsy*. She served in the Australian outback for ten years, hauling all kinds of cargo and supplies, and became VH-MAL in August 1953. *Betsy*'s last operator was Air Queensland.
(*CONAM*)

Silver City Airways was founded in 1946 by an Australian mining group based at Broken Hill (the 'Silver City'). The entire shareholding was bought by Air Commodore G. J. Powell and the British Aviation Services Group in 1948. The airline started the world's first car ferry service, and also operated a number of DC-3s, like G-AMJU (C-47B 43-48664). Juliet Uniform was sold to Zaire as 9Q-CIR on 4 January 1970. (*CONAM*)

Dan-Air Avro York G-ANTK. This ex-RAF C.1 (MW232) was bought by Dan-Air on 16 July 1954. Tango Kilo was finally withdrawn from use and stored at Lasham, Hampshire, in June 1964. It was donated to Lasham Air Scouts as an airfield bunkhouse in October that same year, before it was moved to Duxford Aviation Museum on 23 May 1986 to be preserved. (*CONAM*)

BOAC bought Boeing 377-10-34 Strato-cruiser G-ANUB *RMA Calypso* on 2 September 1954. The aircraft was initially delivered to United Air Lines as N31229 *Mainliner Hilo* on 30 December 1949. Finally, in January 1960, Uniform Bravo was stored at Stansted, Essex, where it was broken up.
(*CONAM*)

During the mid-1950s several aerial work companies were founded in Britain. Dan-Air Services began operations from Blackbushe in 1955. Douglas DC-3s were introduced by companies such as BKS, Derby Airways, Skyways of London and Don Everall Aviation. Pictured are G-AMVC (C-47B 44-77068) of BKS, which operated this Dakota in the early 1950s; G-AMSN (C-47B 44-77047) of Starways, which operated this ex-RAF Dakota from March 1953–March 1954; and G-AMSX of Derby Airways. Victor Charlie (reregistered XF645) crashed on Croglin Fell, Cumbria, on 17 October 1961. Sierra November was last operated in the early 1980s by Pyramid Air Lines, based in Cairo.
(*CONAM*)

Miles/Handley Page Marathon 1A G-AMGW *Millers Dale* was bought by Derby Aviation in October 1955. This aircraft was accepted by West African Airways Corporation as VR-NAN *Lagos* on 28 August 1952, after it was not taken up by BEA as *Clansman*. In July 1960 Golf Whiskey was withdrawn from use and stored at Burnaston, Derbyshire. It was broken up in April 1961.

(*CONAM*)

LOT Polish Airlines Convair 240-12 SP-LPC, seen at Heathrow in 1957, previously served SABENA from 1949 to 1957 as OO-AWS. The CV-240 was the first twin-engined transport to have a pressurised fuselage, and airline orders reached 171 examples. OO-AWS was delivered to SABENA on 30 March 1949. LOT bought the aircraft, reregistered SP-LPC, on 14 October 1957, operating Papa Charlie until 17 January 1966, when it was bought by Westernair of Albuquerque as N656W. This redoubtable Convair was still flying in the 1980s.
(*via Barry Reeve*)

Finnair Convair 340-40 OH-LRB was photographed at London-Heathrow in 1956. The CV-340 differed from the CV-240 in having a fuselage lengthened by 54 inches to include an additional four-seat row in the cabin, an increased wing span, more fuel capacity and more powerful Twin Wasp engines. Airline orders eventually totalled 209 CV-340s. OH-LRB was accepted by Finnair on 15 May 1953 and in 1956 was converted to a CV-440. In November 1980 Romeo Bravo was donated to Suomen Ilmailumuseo.
(*via Barry Reeve*)

Lufthansa Convair 340-68 D-ACIG at Heathrow in 1957. This aircraft was accepted by the German airline on 26 October 1954. It was one of over a hundred CV-340s converted to CV-440 Metropolitans, which introduced various modifications to reduce engine noise and was designed to compete with the Vickers Viscount turboprop airliner. More streamlined cowlings were fitted and the twin tubes of the exhaust were replaced by a rectangular exhaust outlet. D-ACIG was bought by Jugoslovenski Aerotransport as YU-ADP on 17 March 1967. (*via Barry Reeve*)

LEFT: Convair 440-11 Metropolitan HB-IMF *Ticino*, seen at London-Heathrow in 1957, was delivered to Swissair on 1 August 1956. *Ticino* crashed into Mount Laegern, Switzerland, shortly after take-off on a training flight from Kloten Airport on 10 February 1967, killing the four crew.
(*via Barry Reeve*)

BELOW: Swissair's Convair 440-11 HB-IMM *Valais* at Heathrow in 1957. This aircraft was accepted on 28 March 1957. SATA (SA de Transport Aerien) subsequently bought the aircraft on 3 April 1968 and in June it was converted to CV-640 with Rolls-Royce Dart engines replacing the two Twin Wasps. HB-IMM was damaged beyond repair after the undercarriage collapsed whilst landing at Tromsø, Norway, on 17 July 1973.
(*via Barry Reeve*)

Douglas C-54A-15-DC Skymaster CR-IAF *Goa* of TAIP (Transportes Aereos Portugueses Ltd) was initially delivered to the USAAF on 25 August 1944. Post-war, Douglas converted it to DC-4 type and it was bought by United Air Lines on 2 August 1946, as N30059. It was named *Cargoliner Delaware River*, later *Cargoliner Hudson River*.

A total of 1,163 Skymasters was constructed, and 79 civil DC-4s were built post-war. DC-4s and converted C-54s were placed in airline service, beginning in October 1945 with American Overseas Airlines operating flights across the Atlantic. TAIP bought CR-IAF in 1958, and in 1962 it became CS-TDJ. On 30 July this aircraft, now TF-SIF, was bought by the Icelandic Coast Guard. India Foxtrot was withdrawn from use and stored at Seletar, Singapore, in November 1971.
(*GMS*)

It was hoped that the Douglas DC-5, which first flew on 20 February 1939, would prompt large orders from airlines. However, the orders never materialised as problems with excessive tail buffet were revealed during its flight test programme. Only twelve DC-5s were built. The DC-6, however, became one of the world's true greats. It entered fleet operation with both American and United Air Lines on 27 April 1947. Despite early problems, the DC-6 proved very successful and some 704 DC-6, 6A, and 6B versions were built. Some DC-6s continued to serve the smaller airlines until well into the 1980s.

Hunting-Clan Air Transport's Douglas DC-6A/C G-APNO was delivered on 7 August 1958. British United took over Hunting-Clan on 1 July 1960, and in December 1965 November Oscar was transferred to Air Ferry Ltd. Balair bought the aircraft, now registered HB-IBS, on 11 January 1969.
(*GMS*)

United Air Lines DC-7 N6316C *Mainliner Oahu* at Friendship Airport, Baltimore, in June 1958. The DC-7 was a direct development of the DC-6B with the fuselage stretched by 40 inches in order to add one row of seats. All 105 DC-7s built were operated by US trunk carriers, the first beginning service with American Airlines on 4 November 1953. The DC-7 was followed by 112 DC-7Bs and 121 DC-7Cs (Seven Seas), a total production run of 338 aircraft.
(*Walt Truax*)

RIGHT: N6316C was accepted by United Air Lines on 23 September 1954 and later renamed *Mainliner Hartford*. BMR Aviation Ltd was its last operator, buying N6316C on 10 September 1963. (*Walt Truax*)

BELOW: Lockheed produced the Super Constellation by taking the Model 049 and adding new fuselage sections, fore and aft of the wing, to increase tourist-class seating by a third. Some 579 Super Connies were built. L-1049E VT-DHL *Rani of Ajanta* was accepted by Air India on 28 January 1955. It was converted to L-1049G and was bought by the Indian Air Force on 11 June 1962 as BG-580. In December 1983, following service with the Indian Navy as IN-317 (from November 1976), this aircraft was put into storage at Goa. (*CONAM*)

Lockheed L-1049G Super Constellation CS-TLC *Gago Coutinho* of TAP (Transportes Aereos Portugueses) was photographed at London Heathrow in 1958. Lima Charlie was delivered to the airline on 14 September 1955. It was subsequently bought by International Aerodyne on 3 September 1967. After flying with several air cargo companies, N51517 (as it was registered in July 1970) was impounded by the airport authorities at Luqa, Malta, in February 1968 while sporting the spurious registration 5T-TAF and carrying a cargo of aircraft tyres with the suspected destination of Biafra. The Super Connie was auctioned in November 1972 and was later used as a bar in Malta! (*CONAM*)

Douglas DC-7C Seven Seas G-AOIC was delivered to BOAC on 27 November 1956 and was operated until early 1964. India Charlie served a number of airlines until the early 1980s, and was finally broken up in Miami, Florida, in July 1985.
(*CONAM*)

The Douglas DC-7C, the first of which flew on 20 December 1955, had a span 10 feet longer than previous models so it could carry more fuel. It was also the world's first commercial transport able to fly non-stop across the Atlantic in both directions (the DC-7B could not fly non-stop westbound against average winds). The DC-7C entered scheduled service with Pan Am (the airline had set a requirement for such a type) on 1 June 1956. A total of 121 Seven Seas was sold to US and overseas airlines, including BOAC.

G-AOIA, the first of ten DC-7Cs bought by BOAC, was accepted on 23 October 1956. India Alpha was sold in May 1964. After operating in the continental US and Alaska, it was bought by Belize Air Cargo Inc. in January 1979. The Colombian Government seized the aircraft in 1981 and it was used by the Colombian Air Force until it was placed in storage at Bogatá. (*CONAM*)

BOAC took delivery of DC-7C G-AOIE, seen here wearing BEA's famous red squares, on 14 December 1956. India Echo became *County of Perth* in the Caledonian Airways fleet when it was purchased by the Prestwick-based airline on 29 April 1964. Screiner Airways bought the aircraft, now registered PH-SAX, on 9 May 1967. Autair was its last operator, buying the aircraft on 18 November 1969, when it reverted to G-AOIE. (On 1 January 1970, Autair was renamed Court Line.) India Echo was withdrawn from use and stored at Shannon, Eire, in March 1970 and was later used for emergency rescue training at the airport. It is now preserved at Waterford, Eire. (*CONAM*)

Lockheed L-749 Constellation G-ANUZ
Belvedere was purchased by BOAC on 28
February 1955. In the background can be
seen some of BOAC's Stratocruisers.
Uniform Zulu was accepted as PH-TDG
Gouda by KLM on 7 November 1947 and
after conversion to L-749A, was sold to
Capital Airlines on 25 September 1953. In
January 1958 Uniform Zulu was with-
drawn from use and it was stored at
London-Heathrow. After further service
with several US airlines in the 1960s as
N9812F, the aircraft was finally broken up
in 1971.
(*CONAM*)

LEFT: Convair 440-98 OH-VKM, pictured at Heathrow in 1959, was accepted by Kar-Air on 17 June 1954. On 1 March 1964 Kilo Mike was transferred to Finnair, which operated the aircraft until April 1973. After flying with Key Airlines and Basler Flight Service, the aircraft, now N357SA, was leased by Salair in 1987. It crashed shortly after take-off from Santo Domingo, Dominican Republic, on 27 June 1995. (*via Barry Reeve*)

BELOW: Bristol 170 Mk 21 Freighter G-AIMH was registered by the Ministry of Civil Aviation on 3 December 1946, and was accepted by Cie Air Transport as F-BECT on 10 December 1948. Silver City Airways bought Charlie Tango on 1 April 1952, and named it *City of Birmingham* in 1959. Manx Airlines bought Mike Hotel on 6 November 1961. It was withdrawn from use and stored at Lydd, Kent, in October 1962, and was finally broken up in 1963. (*CONAM*)

Silver City Airways had been formed at Lympne airfield near Folkestone in summer 1948 to ferry cars between England and Le Touquet in northern France. By 1954 its fleet had expanded to six Freighters and nine Superfreighters, or 'Frighteners' as these aircraft were popularly known. Silver City Airways was one of five independent aviation companies which were merged to form British United Airways in 1962.
(*CONAM*)

ABOVE: Indian Princess. Lockheed L-1049G Super Constellation VT-DJX *Rani of Saguri* was accepted by Air India on 13 August 1958. In August 1960 this Super Connie was converted to a freighter, renamed The Flying Sherpa and then on 16 January 1962 it was bought by the Indian Air Force as BG-579. (*CONAM*)

LEFT: Lockheed L-749 G-ANUP on lease to Skyways of London *circa* 1959. This Constellation was accepted by QANTAS as VH-EAA *Ross Smith* on 4 October 1947. Converted to L-479A, the aircraft, now registered as G-ANUP and named *Branksome*, was bought by BOAC on 15 February 1955. Uniform Papa was put into storage at London-Heathrow in September 1957 and then leased, in September 1959, to Skyways. The airline operated G-ANUP until April 1962, when it was returned to BOAC. Aero Transport bought the aircraft, now OE-IFO, on 10 May 1963. Interocean bought the aircraft in July 1964 as LX-IOK. On 2 October 1964 it was damaged beyond repair after it veered off the runway at Addis Ababa, Ethiopia. (*CONAM*)

Vickers Viking 657/1 G-AGRS of Orion Airways Ltd, which bought this aircraft on 1 July 1959. G-AGRS first flew on 28 June 1946 and was accepted by BOAC on 9 July 1946. Romeo Sierra later served with BEA and British South American Airways Corporation, and was converted from 498/1A to Type 657/1. As VP-TAV, this aircraft was operated by British West Indian Airways and was named *Jamaica*. Whilst in Eagle Airways' service (1957–59) G-AGRS was more grandly known as *Lord Charles Beresford*. (Eagle Airways became Cunard Eagle Airways on 5 January 1961.) G-AGRS was last used, on lease, by Air Safaris in August 1961. It was finally broken up at Southend, Essex, in May 1963.
(*CONAM*)

Canadair Ltd developed a Rolls-Royce Merlin-powered version of the C-54 Skymaster, initially for the RCAF (as North Stars), and for Trans Canada Airlines (TCA). TCA introduced an unpressurised RCAF version DC-4M-I, on loan, on its Montreal–London route on 15 April 1947. Twenty pressurised versions were delivered between October 1947 and June 1948. Canadian Pacific Air Lines took delivery of four C-4s between May and July 1949. BOAC ordered twenty-two Canadair C-4s powered by four 1,760 hp Merlin 626s to replace the unsuccessful Avro Tudors on its Empire routes. C-4s in BOAC service became known as the Argonaut class. Deliveries took place between March and November 1949, and services began on the London–Pakistan–India–Far East route.

G-ALHP *Aethra* was accepted by BOAC on 2 September 1949. Overseas Aviation bought Hotel Papa on 12 June 1959, and in October 1961 it went to Derby Airways to be used for spares before being broken up.
(*CONAM*)

Sent to Coventry. Trans European Airways Bristol Freighter Mk I G-AGPV at Coventry *circa* 1960. This aircraft was converted to a Wayfarer in October 1947, two years after the Bristol Aeroplane Company registered the aircraft after it was not taken up by the Ministry of Supply. Trans European purchased Papa Victor on 17 November 1960 and leased it to North South Airlines in July 1961. G-AGPV was stored at Bagington, Coventry, in July 1963 and then broken up at Gatwick Airport in September 1965.
(*CONAM*)

Canadair C-4 Argonaut G-ALHV *Adonis*, one of seventy C-4s built, was accepted by BOAC on 7 October 1949. In April 1960, BOAC finally withdrew its last Argonauts. G-ALHV was bought by Aden Airways in June 1960 as VR-AAT. The next owner, Derby Airways, bought the aircraft in December 1963. When Hotel Victor was withdrawn from use it was used for spares at Burnaston, Derbyshire. (*GMS*)

Messenger of the Gods. Handley Page Hermes IV G-ALDL of Air Safaris in 1961. Between 1954 and 1958 (prior to the introduction of the Comet 4 jetliner), the Bristol Hercules-powered Hermes proved, once severe early teething troubles were rectified, to be one of BOAC's most comfortable airliners.

G-ALDL first flew on 9 February 1951 and was accepted by BOAC on 6 March as *Hector*. BOAC took delivery of twenty Hermes IVs which were operated until the end of 1954. (Five overweight Hermes IVs were rejected.) Delta Lima was later converted to a IVA, and on 9 May 1955 was one of ten Hermes bought by Skyways,

before being returned to Hermes IV type with the refitting of Hercules 773s using lower-grade fuel than the original 763s. Air Safaris bought G-ALDL on 16 May 1961 but its use there was short, for on 9 November it was repossessed by Skyways. Delta Lima was broken up in August 1962. (*CONAM*)

All Nippon Airways (ANA) Convair 440-89 JA5055, pictured in 1961. This aircraft was accepted by the airline on 29 October 1957 and it was used by ANA until 1965, when it was bought by General Dynamics Corporation and converted to CV-640. After operating with Hawaiian Airlines on lease, N45004 as it had now become, was bought by Pacific Western Airlines as CF-PWS on 27 February 1967. After further operation with Gateway Aviation and Time Air as C-FPWS, the aircraft was withdrawn from use and stored at Springbank, Alberta, in December 1991. (*via Barry Reeve*)

Capitol Airways Lockheed L-1049E on finals circa 1961. This Super Connie was accepted by QANTAS as VH-EAE Southern Moon on 6 February 1955. In 1958 Alpha Echo was converted to L-1049G and on 2 March 1960 was bought by Lockheed as N9720C. Capitol leased the aircraft in May 1961 and purchased it outright in December that year. N9720C was finally scrapped in 1970.
(*CONAM*)

Douglas DC-4-1009 G-AOXK of British United Airways in the early 1960s. This aircraft was accepted by SAS as OY-DFI *Dan Viking* on 6 May 1946. Air Charter bought the aircraft, now G-AOXK, on 8 October 1956, and named it *Golden Fleece*. Air Charter was merged to form BUA on 1 July 1960, and in July 1963 X-Ray Kilo was bought by Aviation Traders Ltd. Its next owner was Williamson Diamond Mines, and after further service, with Zaire Aero Service in 1977, it was withdrawn from use and stored.
(*CONAM*)

Imperial Airlines Lockheed L-049 N2737A in 1961. This Constellation was accepted by BOAC as G-AHEK *Berwick* on 21 May 1946. In 1952 Echo Kilo was converted to L-049D, and in July 1953 it was converted again, this time to L-049E. Capital Airlines bought the aircraft on 27 February 1955 and on 14 April 1961 N2737A was sold to Miami Aircraft & Engine Sales. Imperial Airlines leased the aircraft on 2 May 1961 and bought it on 14 July. N2737A crashed while making an emergency landing at Byrd Airport, at Richmond, Virginia, on 8 November 1961, with the loss of seventy-seven people on board.
(*CONAM*)

ABOVE: Douglas DC-6A G-ARMY of Cunard Eagle Airways. The airline bought Mike Yankee, previously VR-BBP, on 23 March 1961. Cunard Eagle (from October 1963 renamed British Eagle) reregistered the aircraft G-ARMY on 16 May 1961. It was acquired by Slick Airways as N7818C on 23 April 1958. Its last operators were Saudi Arabian Airlines, which bought the aircraft, now registered HZ-ADB, on 26 March 1964, and Yemen Airways, when it was reregistered 4W-ABP. In 1982 it was withdrawn from use and stored at Sana'a, Yemen.
(*CONAM*)

RIGHT: Overseas Aviation Douglas DC-43M2 CF-TFK North Star with most of its rudder missing. This aircraft was accepted by Trans Canada Airlines as '211' on 14 February 1948. Overseas Aviation bought Foxtrot Kilo on 1 July 1961. Following Keegan Aviation Ltd's purchase of the aircraft, it was withdrawn from use and stored at Bagington, Coventry, before being broken up.
(*GMS*)

Lockheed L-749A Constellation G-ANUR was leased by Skyways of London in July 1959, and then bought outright on 2 July 1962. Initially accepted by QANTAS as VH-EAB *Lawrence Hargrave* on 8 October 1947, it was sold to BOAC in 1955 and renamed *Basildon.* Following service with Britannia Airways (1964–66), Uniform Romeo was reregistered and it was finally broken up at Montevideo, Uruguay. (*CONAM*)

Canadian Queen. Douglas DC-6B G-ARXZ on lease to British United Airways in 1962. This aircraft was accepted by Canadian Pacific Airlines (CPA) as CF-CZS on 30 April 1957 and named *Empress of Montreal*. BUA leased this aircraft on 24 March 1962, returning X-Ray Zulu to CPA on 30 September 1964, when it was renamed *Empress of Lisbon*. This aircraft was converted to DC-6A/B in 1965, and given a new name, *Empress of Edmonton*. Zulu Sierra was sold to Transair Ltd in March 1969, and then reregistered OY-DRM when Greenlandair bought it on 16 June 1972. The empress's reign over, it was renamed *Suluik*. Air Atlantique bought the aircraft, now G-SIXA, in May 1979. X-Ray Alpha was withdrawn from use and stored at Manston, Kent, before being broken up in April 1985.
(*CONAM*)

ABOVE: Douglas DC-3 (C-47B 44-77249) EC-ATM was leased to TASSA, from 27 November 1962 to 2 November 1963. This Dakota served in the RAF during the Second World War and was bought by BEA as G-AMNV on 16 January 1952. On 20 June 1962 November Victor was sold to Tyne Tees Air Charter Ltd. This Dakota was later operated by several carriers, including Swedeair, Autair, Air Senegal and Bechuanaland Natal. Its last role was performing aerial survey work in Botswana.
(GMS)

LEFT: AT(E)L.98 Carvair LX-IOH of Interocean Airways was photographed in Malaysia in 1963. The Carvair was a modified C-54 development, and some twenty-one second-hand C-54s and DC-4-1009 airframes were delivered by Aviation Traders (Engineering) Ltd between 1960 and 1968. The first Carvair went into service with Channel Air Bridge on its scheduled Southend–Rotterdam service on 1 March 1962. LX-IOH first flew on 5 September 1962 and it was delivered to Intercontinental US Inc. on 20 September 1962. Interocean Airways bought Oscar Hotel in January 1963 and operated it for two years. The aircraft was then bought by CIE Air Transport on 19 June 1965 registered F-BMHU and named *Cdt Heri de Montal*. Hotel Uniform crashed onto the main road after taking off from Karachi, Pakistan, on 8 March 1967, killing the four crew and seven on the ground.
(Jerry Cullum)

Lockheed L-1049G Super Constellation F-BHBI was delivered to Air France on 23 February 1956. Bravo India was bought by Air Fret on 5 April 1968. Phoenix Air Transport acquired the aircraft in June 1969 and leased it to the Biafran Government. In January 1970 Bravo India was stored at Arecife in the Canary Islands. The aircraft was destroyed by fire in 1984. (*GMS*)

Capitol International Airlines Lockheed L-1049H N1927H in the early 1960s. This Super Connie was leased to Transocean Air Lines on 17 July 1957 and from April 1959 was leased by Capitol. Capitol then bought N1927H in 1964 and operated the airliner for four years. Canairelief bought the aircraft, now registered CF-AEN, in November 1969. Echo November was broken up in June 1974. (*GMS*)

South African Airways (SAA) Douglas DC-7B ZS-DKE *Reiger* in November 1963. This aircraft, one of four DC-7Bs acquired by SAA, was accepted by the airline on 2 March 1956. Kilo Echo was converted to DC-7BF in 1968, and bought by TAN Airlines in May 1969. The aircraft was broken up at Miami, Florida, in May 1971. (*CONAM*)

Douglas DC-4 (C-54B-1-DC) LX-IOA, owned by Interocean Airways. This aircraft was delivered to the USAAF as 42-72329 on 23 October 1944. Post-war, it was converted to DC-4 configuration and on 25 March 1946 it was accepted by United Air Lines as N30045 *Mainliner Crater Lake*. Transocean Air Lines bought N30045 on 26 November 1956, and after being leased to Iranian Airways, it was purchased by Intercontinental in April 1960. On 1 July 1960 Interocean Airways bought this aircraft, now LX-IOA, operating it until 2 May 1966. In April 1968, this aircraft, now N90440, was impounded and stored at Frankfurt, West Germany. In October 1968 it was bought by Transportflug as D-ABOW. The next owner was SODEMAC, which bought the aircraft, now 9Q-CTE, on 6 October 1970. In 1981 it was withdrawn from use and stored. (*GMS*)

Douglas C-54A-DO Skymaster YK-ADA of Syrian Arab at London-Heathrow in the early 1960s. This aircraft, which was first delivered to the USAAF on 16 September 1943, was damaged beyond repair after overrunning the runway while landing at Damascus, Syria, on 2 October 1964. (*GMS*)

Irish King. Douglas DC-4 EI-APK *Monarch of Munster* on lease to Alitalia in the 1960s. This aircraft was delivered to Northwest Airlines on 9 March 1946. It was then bought by Trek Airways in April 1958, and was renamed *Louis Trichardt*. Reregistered as LX-SAF, it joined Luxair's fleet on 1 December 1961, and was renamed *Ville de Luxembourg*. In May 1964 Universal Trading Corporation bought the aircraft and leased it to Shannon Air as EI-ANL on 30 May 1964. Alitalia then leased it in October 1965. In February 1966, the aircraft was impounded by the British Airports Authority, and was returned to Universal Trading Corporation in March. Aer Turas bought the aircraft, now EI-APK, in December 1966, operating it for three years. At the end of this period it was reregistered N6304D. In February 1977 the aircraft was withdrawn from use and stored at Hal Far, Malta. Transferred to the 'fire dump' in 1983, it was broken up in 1985.
(*GMS*)

Douglas DC-3 (C-47 41-18349) 7T-VBB of Afric Air at Toulouse, France, sometime in 1965–66. This ex-USAAF C-47 served in the 8th Air Force in England in May 1942 and in the 12th Air Force in Italy. It was bought by LAI in April 1947 as I-LUCE. Alitalia bought the aircraft in November 1957. In December 1959 TAI purchased the aircraft, now F-BJUT, and in October 1961 Uniform Tango was sold to Air Inter. It was bought by Air Atlantique in January 1963, and was then sold to SACA (Afric Air) in February 1965. It was derelict at Toulouse in August 1966.
(*GMS*)

OPPOSITE AND ABOVE: Airspeed AS.57 Ambassador 2 G-AMAH of Dan-Air undergoing repairs to the port Bristol Centaurus engine in October 1967. Alpha Hotel was the last of the twenty-three Ambassadors built, twenty-one of which were originally for British European Airways Corporation. Aircraft that flew for this airline were known as the 'Elizabethan class' and had names like *William Shakespeare*, *Sir Walter Raleigh* and *Lord Burghley*. The latter aircraft (G-ALZU) crashed on take-off at Munich on 6 February 1958. The death toll finally reached twenty-three, seven of whom were members of the famous Manchester United 'Busby Babes' football team.

Alpha Hotel had been accepted by BEA as *Sir Christopher Hatton* on 6 March 1953. Butler Air Transport then bought the aircraft on 6 June 1957 and it was reregistered as VH-BUJ on 2 August. On 14 November 1958, Dan-Air bought the aircraft, and reregistered it G-AMAH on 12 November 1959. Alpha Hotel was stored in March 1971 and finally broken up in 1972. (*Stan Lee*)

ABOVE: Air Cameroun Lockheed L-1049 F-BGNI, which was accepted by Air France on 25 October 1953, pictured on lease in March 1968. Six years earlier the Super Constellation had been converted to a freighter. F-BGNI returned to Air France in October 1971, and after being stored at Nîmes-Garons, it was broken up in 1975. (*GMS*)

RIGHT: Pacific Northern Airlines Lockheed L-749A N6017C in summer 1968. This Constellation was accepted by TWA on 21 December 1950, and named *Star of the District of Columbia* '817'. After operating on lease to other airlines in the early 1960s, N6017C was bought by Pacific Northern on 1 October 1963. It was finally broken up in 1971 in Panama. (*GMS*)

Douglas DC-7 G-ATAB of Dan-Air in April 1968. This aircraft was accepted by United Air Lines as N6348C *Mainliner Akron Canton* on 30 September 1957. It was converted to DC-7BF in December 1960. Trans World Leasing purchased it on Christmas Eve 1964, registered as G-ATAB. Dan-Air leased the aircraft in March 1966 and then bought G-ATAB outright in December 1966. Alpha Bravo was so often covered in oil that the aircraft was reportedly referred to as the 'Torrey Canyon'! G-ATAB was stored at Lasham, Hampshire, in June 1969 and finally broken up in August 1973. (*Stan Lee*)

British United Douglas DC-3 (C-53D 42-68784) G-AOBN. In the early post-war years this aircraft was operated by ABA and SAS in Sweden and by several French carriers, until 20 May 1965 when it was bought by Air Cruise. Silver City bought Bravo November on 28 October 1957. British United operated Bravo November from 1 October 1962 until 1 October 1968, when the carrier was renamed BUIA. G-AOBN went on to operate with BIA, Air Anglia and Air Freight (Lydd).
(*CONAM*)

LEFT: Sterling Airways Douglas DC-6B OY-STT. This aircraft was accepted by Northwest Orient Airlines as N579 on 23 January 1958. Following service with Northwest Orient Airlines, United Arab and Yemen Airways, Sterling bought the aircraft on 10 June 1968. OY-STT became SE-ENZ with Sterling Sweden on 10 July 1971.
(*CONAM*)

BELOW: Intertrade Leasing Corporation Lockheed L-1049H N469C. This Super Constellation was accepted as N6636C by California Eastern Aviation on 24 July 1958. That same year it operated on lease with Transcontinental SA, as LV-FTV, and in the 1960s it was leased by other operators, including Slick Airways, LEBCA and Air Mid East. In 1968 N469C was withdrawn from use and stored at Sebring, Florida, before being broken up.
(*GMS*)

North TAN Airlines Douglas DC-7B HR-TNK in December 1968. This aircraft was accepted by Pan Am, registered as N51703, on 25 August 1955. Ten years later it was converted to DC-7BF. In 1967 it was operated by Braniff, although North TAN Airlines bought N51703 later that same year. Three years later, the aircraft was finally broken up in Miami, Florida.
(*GMS*)

Lockheed L-1049 N6237G of Eastern Air Lines in January 1969. This Super Constellation was accepted by Eastern on 2 November 1956. California Airmotive Corporation bought the aircraft on 30 September 1968 and it was then broken up in 1971 at Lancaster, California.
(*GMS*)

Lockheed L-1049G N9751C of Trans International Airlines in January 1969. This Super Constellation was delivered to QANTAS as VH-EAD *Southern Dawn* on 18 November 1955. TIA bought the aircraft on 3 September 1964 and used it until July 1968 when it was put into storage at Oakland, California. N9751C was broken up at Fox Field, Lancaster, California, in November 1969.
(*GMS*)

Royal Air Cambodge Douglas DC-6B XU-IAJ at Hong Kong's Kai Tak Airport in January 1969. This aircraft was accepted by Trans American Airlines as N3024C on 20 March 1957. Airnautic bought the aircraft, now F-BJKZ, on 1 June 1962. It was leased to Royal Air Cambodge from July 1966 until 1974, when it was bought by the French *l'Armée de l'Air*, who used it until 1980.
(*GMS*)

Lockheed L-1049H PP-YSB of VARIG. This Super Constellation was accepted by REAL SA on 17 February 1958, then transferred to VARIG in August 1961. Carolina Aircraft Corporation bought PP-YSB, now N564E, on 23 September 1969. After operating on lease with Gulf Export-Import Inc., in 1970, N564E was bought by Balair Inc. on 15 February 1971. It crashed into the sea south of Great Inagua, Bahamas, on 20 October 1971.
(*GMS*)

Lockheed L-1049H N565E in March 1969. This Super Constellation was accepted by REAL SA, as PP-YSC *Brasilia*, on 20 February 1958. It was then transferred to VARIG in August 1961. After operating with Carolina Aircraft Corporation, Flying W Airways and Produce International, N565E was broken up at Fort Lauderdale, Florida, in 1972.
(*GMS*)

Universal Airlines Douglas DC-6 N6574C in April 1969. This aircraft was accepted by KLM, as PH-TGA *Dr Ir M. H. Damme*, on 18 July 1953. On 12 May 1960, Nevada Aero Trades bought the aircraft, now N6574C, and leased it to various continental US and Alaskan operators. The aircraft's next owners were Twentieth Century Aircraft, which bought it in 1963, and Zantop Air Transport, which purchased it on 19 June 1964. Two years later, Zantop was renamed Universal Airlines. Span East Air Lines bought the aircraft, now registered N611SE, in January 1970, and in August 1971 Alcon bought the aircraft, now CP-947 and named *Tigre*. It was damaged beyond repair whilst landing at San Juan, Bolivia, on 6 February 1974. (*GMS*)

Douglas DC-6 (C-54D-10-DC) N403US of USDA (Air Distribution) in April 1969. This aircraft was accepted by the USAAF on 20 August 1945 as 42-72764. It went on to serve with China Airlines, the US Civil Air Transport, Air Asia and Air America. Air Distribution bought the aircraft on 30 November 1973. Air Asia was its last operator, from 25 February 1976, before it was put into storage in September 1977. (*GMS*)

Dan-Air Airspeed AS.57 Ambassador 2 G-ALZO at Tarbes, in south-western France, was photographed in October 1969. Zebra Oscar was accepted by BEA on 25 November 1952 and named *Christopher Marlowe*. The Royal Jordanian Air Force bought G-ALZO on 20 May 1960, and Zebra Oscar was then purchased by Handley Page Ltd on 1 February 1963.

Dan-Air acquired the aircraft on 26 February 1963. In September 1971, G-ALZO was withdrawn from use and stored at Lasham, Hampshire. It was preserved and then taken by road to Duxford on 25 October 1993. (Dan-Air ceased operations on 23 October 1992.) (*Stan Lee*)

ABOVE: Convair 440-86 N9303 in April 1969 when it was leased by Standard Airways. This aircraft was accepted by Eastern Air Lines as '303' on 17 April 1957. Standard leased N9303 from 27 March 1969 to 1970, when it returned to Eastern Air Lines. Mackey International Airlines bought N9303 in March 1972, and reregistered it N443JM in 1974. The aircraft was later withdrawn from use and stored at Fort Lauderdale.
(*GMS*)

RIGHT: Douglas DC-6 N90705 of Holiday in April 1969. This aircraft was delivered to American Airlines as *Flagship Arizona* on 14 March 1947. In September 1979 N90705 was withdrawn from use and stored at Fort Lauderdale, Florida, before being broken up.
(*GMS*)

ATL.98 Carvair G-AXAI first flew on 2 April 1969, and was accepted by British Air Ferries on the same day. In 1972 Alpha India was named *Fat Albert*. In January 1976, now registered F-BVEF, it was bought by SECMAFER. It went to the United States in 1979 as N55243, and after operating with Pacific Air Express and Academy Airlines, it was broken up in Florida in 1992.
(*British World Airlines*)

Lockheed L-1049H N6931C in July 1969. This Super Connie was accepted by California Eastern Aviation on 18 April 1957. It was operated by many carriers, until it was damaged beyond repair in an emergency landing at Guadaloupe on 3 June 1975, whilst flying for Sky Truck International. In 1979 N6931C was broken up, and the nose section went to the *Musée de L'Air*. (*GMS*)

LEFT: Germanair Douglas DC-6A D-ABAY in May 1969. This aircraft was accepted by Flying Tiger Line on 17 August 1953 as N34954. In August 1953 Japan Air Lines bought the aircraft, now JA6203 and named *City of Nara*. After operation with Transavia Holland in 1968, Germanair bought the aircraft that October. In 1971 Alpha Yankee was put into storage in Switzerland but this was not permanent as it was later used by several airlines. (*GMS*)

BELOW: Lockheed L-1049H EC-ARN *Santiago* of Iberia in the mid-sixties. This Super Constellation was accepted by Thai Airways on 24 September 1957. It was next used as XA-NAF by Guest Aerovias Mexico. Iberia bought this aircraft, now EC-ARN, in February 1962, and in October 1964 converted it to a freighter version. International Aerodyne bought Romeo November in May 1967 and the following year leased it to RAPSA (RA PANAMENAS) Ltd, where the aircraft operated as HP-467. A fire in engine number three caused the aircraft to crash after take-off from Panama City on 30 March 1968, with the loss of the three crew. (*GMS*)

RIGHT: Transair Sweden Super DC-7B SE-ERG *Halsingborg*. This aircraft was accepted by Eastern Air Lines on 12 December 1957, then was sold to Transair Sweden AB on 10 August 1965. Romeo Golf was put into storage at Malmö, Sweden, in August 1968 and then broken up the following year. (*GMS*)

BELOW: Lockheed L-1049D N6502C *Zurich Airtrader* of Seaboard and Western Airlines was photographed whilst on finals in July 1969. This Super Constellation was accepted by Seaboard and Western Airlines on 2 September 1954. It was converted to L-1049H in 1956 and continued to serve with this carrier until 1962, when it was bought by Canadair. N6502C was finally broken up in August 1967. (*GMS*)

Lockheed L-1049H N6924C of Flying Tiger
Line starting its engines in July 1969. On
15 October 1978, whilst operating with an
unknown airline, this Super Constellation
crashed on take-off from Riohacha,
Colombia.
(*GMS*)

Douglas DC-3 (C-47A-1-DK 42-92399) G-AGJV of British Midland with an Airspeed Ambassador in the background. Juliet Victor was operated by BOAC and BEA in the immediate post-war years and it also served Pionair and Derby Aviation before being bought by BMA on 1 October 1964. Air Evoy acquired G-AGJV on 22 March 1969 and Juliet Victor was then bought by Air Ulster on 7 July 1969. Air Anglia bought the aircraft in February 1972 and it joined the Air Freight (Lydd) fleet in November 1975. In February 1980, Air BVI (its last operator) bought the aircraft, now VP-LVM, from Skyways Cargo. (*CONAM*)

SABENA DC-7C OO-SFC in 1969. This aircraft was delivered to SABENA on 20 December 1956. It was converted to DC-7CF in 1969, and leased to Spantax SA in 1967. Spantax SA bought the aircraft, now EC-BSQ, in January 1970. In 1979 it was withdrawn from use and stored at Las Palmas, in the Canary Islands, and is now used by the airport authority (AENA). (*GMS*)

Douglas DC-6 HK-754 of Aerocondor Colombia. This aircraft was accepted by KLM on 15 March 1948, as PH-TPI, and named *Prinses Irene*. Linn Aeronautica SA bought the aircraft, now PH-DPI, on 21 January 1964. Two months later, Aerocondor Colombia bought the aircraft, now CF-TFK. In July 1970 Foxtrot Kilo was bought by Aerocosta Colombia and in October it was converted to DC-6F. The aircraft was broken up two years later. (*CONAM*)

RIGHT: Air Nevada (formerly Hawthorne Nevada Airlines) L-049 Constellation N9412H in February 1970. After serving with Executive Party Club and Produce Custom Air Freight, this aircraft was bought on 23 May 1976 by Frank Lembo Enterprises Inc. and turned into a restaurant at Greenwood Lake, New Jersey. Thirty years earlier, on 13 June 1946, the aircraft was accepted by Air France, registered as F-BAZA. For over twenty years, until Hawthorne Nevada Airlines bought it on 3 June 1968, N9412H was operated by many carriers, including Transcontinental & Western Air, which named it *Star of the Azores*. Whilst in Royal Air Burundi service, in 1962, it went under the less memorable name of *Umuganwa Luodvika Rwagasore*! (*GMS*)

Pacific Air Transport Lockheed L-049 N90816 in February 1970. This Constellation was a sister ship of N9412H at Transcontinental & Western Air, and was named *Star of Geneva*. It was delivered to this airline (which was renamed Trans World Airlines on 17 May 1950) on 25 September 1946. N90816 was finally broken up in June 1990. (*GMS*)

Capitol International Airlines Lockheed L-749A N4901C, pictured in February 1970. The aircraft was to have become *Star of Colorado* in TWA service, but it was not taken up by the airline. Instead, this Connie was accepted on 25 June 1951 as N6025C by Hughes Tool Company. On 23 September 1954, BOAC bought the L-749A, now registered G-ANNT and named *Buckingham*. Capitol stepped in and bought the aircraft, now N4901C, on 25 March 1958. In March 1970 Capitol donated this aircraft, now N6695C, to the Aeronautical Historical Association, which put it on display at Bradley Air Museum, Connecticut. It was destroyed by a tornado on 3 October 1979. (*GMS*)

Air Viet Nam Douglas DC-4 (C-54D-15-DC) XV-NUI in February 1970. This aircraft was delivered to the USAAF as 43-17224 on 31 August 1945. In 1966 Air Viet Nam bought the aircraft, now registered N553. On 19 March 1973 XV-NUI crashed near Ben Me Thuot, 290 kilometres north of Saigon, South Vietnam, after an explosion in the cargo area, killing fifty-nine people on board. (*GMS*)

TWA Lockheed L-1649A Starliner N7310C *Star of Kansas* in February 1970. The prototype Starliner flew on 10 October 1956. The type could fly non-stop from New York to any European capital and went into service with TWA on the New York to Paris route on 1 June 1957. Some forty-three production models were built between 1957 and 1966, twenty-nine being ordered by TWA, ten by Air France and four by Lufthansa. N7310C was delivered to the Hughes Tool Company on 28 May 1957 and then bought by TWA on 19 December that year. In September 1966, after further service with Delta, Charlotte Aircraft Corporation and Alaska Airlines, it was finally broken up for spares. (*GMS*)

Lockheed L-1049H Super Constellation N1006C, with Seaboard & World Airlines' lettering on the empennage, at New York in February 1970. N1006C was accepted by Seaboard and Western Airlines as *Prestwick Airtrader* on 5 December 1956 and was sold to Capitol Airways on 31 December 1965. N1006C was stored in July 1972, and finally broken up in 1975. (*GMS*)

Douglas DC-6B N90961 of Continental Airlines at New York–La Guardia. In the foreground is the wing of DC-6 N37540 *Mainliner New Jersey*, which was delivered to United Airlines on 28 August 1948. N90961 was accepted by Continental on 5 January 1955, and was leased to Air Micronesia on 16 May 1968. It was withdrawn from use in 1975 and stored at Oakland, California. Converted to DC-6BF, it was then sold to Aerospace Products Inc. in November 1978. It was later impounded, at El Dorado, Bogatá, Colombia, in August 1979.
(*GMS*)

Aviateca Guatemala Douglas DC-6 TG-AHA *Xelaju*. This aircraft was accepted by Braniff Airways on 3 November 1947 and subsequently bought by Aviateca on 5 February 1966. It was put into storage in 1979.
(*GMS*)

Fred Olsen's Flyselskap Air Service bought C-46A-45-CU LN-FOS on 18 November 1957, and after conversion to C-46R, it was sold to Continental Air Services on 29 June 1971. Oscar Sierra, which was initially delivered to the USAAF on 13 July 1944, was finally withdrawn from use and stored at Seletar, Singapore, in November 1978. (*GMS*)

Icelandair Douglas DC-6B TF-FIP *Solfaxi* in October 1970. This aircraft was accepted by SAS as LN-LML *Heming Viking* on 4 July 1952. Mike Lima was then leased to Thai International on 27 April 1960 as *Thepsatri*, before returning to SAS on 29 June 1963. Icelandair bought the aircraft, now TF-FIP, on 4 January 1964. The next owner, Delta Air Transport, bought the aircraft, now OO-RVG, on 10 April 1972. In November 1973 the aircraft, now N3549H, was converted to DC-6BF. It was sold to Conifair Aviation in March 1990. (*GMS*)

Douglas DC-6B OO-CTL on lease to Sobelair in 1970. This aircraft was accepted by SABENA on 6 May 1953. OO-CTL was damaged beyond repair at Malaga, Spain, on 20 December 1970. (*GMS*)

Douglas DC-6B SE-ENY of Sterling Airways, which bought the ex-Northwest Orient Airlines aircraft on 15 February 1964 as OY-BAT and reregistered it as SE-ENY on 15 March 1971. November Yankee was withdrawn from use and stored at Copenhagen-Kastrup, Denmark, in March 1972. It later flew with Conair Aviation as C-GHCA, until it was finally put into storage at Abbotsford, Canada. (*CONAM*)

Sorry-looking Connie. Ghana-registered Lockheed L-1049G 9G-28 *Fleche des Almadies* sitting derelict at Fox Field, California, was broken up in March 1971. This Super Constellation was accepted by Trans Canada Air Lines on 20 December 1957. It was destined to operate with Cyprus Airways as *Archbishop Makarios III* in 1966, but it was not taken up. (*Tony Hudson*)

Lockheed L-1649A N179AV in Air Venturers livery in January 1972. This Starliner was accepted by Lufthansa as D-ALAN *Neckar* on 20 December 1957. In July 1960 Alpha November was converted to a freighter. Air Venturers of Houston Inc., bought the aircraft, now N179AV, on 10 March 1966.
(*GMS*)

Douglas DC-6BF HP-523 *Ciudad de Colon* of Inair Panama in May 1972. This aircraft was accepted by Pan Am as DC-6B N6524C *Clipper Pocahontas* on 19 April 1952. It was later renamed *Clipper Essen*, and finally, *Clipper Meteor*. In March 1968, N6524C was put into storage in Miami, Florida. It was then bought by Inair Panama, registered HP-503, on 12 March 1970. In April 1975 HP-503 was converted to DC-6BF.
(*GMS*)

RIGHT: Virgin Islands Air Cargo Douglas DC-6B N4061K was photographed in June 1972. This aircraft was accepted by Pan Am as N4061K *Clipper Dawn* on 8 July 1953. It was sold to Aaxio Airlines on 30 June 1964 and in November it was converted to DC-6BF. Virgin Islands Air Cargo leased the aircraft in January 1972. (*GMS*)

BELOW: AFISA (Aerofletes Internacionales) Lockheed L-1049H HP526 *Orula* in November 1972. This Super Constellation was accepted by Flying Tiger Line as N6917C '807' on 9 April 1957. Whilst operating on lease to ANDES on 16 December 1973, N6917C suffered overrotation due to improper cargo loading. It crashed four kilometres east of Miami shortly after take-off, killing the three crew and six people on the ground. (*GMS*)

SAM Colombia Douglas C-54B-1-DC HK-528 in February 1973. This aircraft was delivered to the USAAF on 27 November 1944. Post-war, it was bought by Douglas and converted to DC-4, before being bought by Pan Am on 17 July 1946 as *Clipper Black Warrior*. It later served with Eastern Air Lines and Trans Equipment Company before being bought by SAM Colombia in 1968. HK-528 was sold to Aerotabo Colombia, later renamed Aertolineas Medellín, in 1974. Finally, HK-528 was broken up in 1988.
(*GMS*)

Lockheed L-1049H CF-AEN in Hellenic Air
Ltd livery in February 1973. This Super
Connie was leased to Transocean Air Lines
on 17 July 1957, before being bought by the
Babb Company Inc. in April 1959. Canairelief bought the aircraft, now CF-AEN,
in November 1969. Hellenic Air Ltd was
set to buy the aircraft in 1970 but it was
not taken up. CF-AEN was stored at St
Hubert, Canada, in April 1971 and finally
broken up in June 1974.
(*GMS*)

LEFT: Compania Dominicana Douglas DC-6B HI-92 in February 1973. This aircraft was accepted by Pan Am as N6532C *Clipper Aurora* on 31 August 1952. Compania Dominicana bought the aircraft, now HI-92, on 6 March 1964. HI-92 was converted to DC-6BF in May 1975. Eventually, it was withdrawn from use and stored at Santo Domingo, Dominican Republic, in January 1982.
(*GMS*)

BELOW: LACSA Douglas DC-6B TI-1018C *Cariari* in February 1973. This aircraft was accepted by Pan Am as N6530C *Clipper Pathfinder* on 22 August 1952. In August 1960 the aircraft was renamed *Clipper Frankfurt* and in 1962 it was converted to DC-6A/B. LACSA bought the aircraft, now TI-1018C, on 1 September 1963. Its last owner was Angel Arciero, who bought it from SAISA in February 1987. The airliner was impounded at Merida, Mexico, the same year.
(*GMS*)

Guyana Airways Douglas DC-6A N610SE was photographed whilst undergoing engine maintenance in 1974. This aircraft was accepted by Slick Airways as N90807 *Miss Judy* on 17 September 1951. From 24 March 1953 to June 1968 it was operated by JAL, as JA6201 *City of Tokyo*. In the 1970s this aircraft was operated by several carriers, then bought by Span East Airlines on 7 September 1973, which leased it to Guyana Airways in January 1974. The aircraft was reregistered 8R-GEC by Guyana. It was returned to Span East Airlines on 31 July 1976.
(*GMS*)

British Air Ferries AT(E)L.98 Carvair G-ASDC *Big Louie*, viewed through the port propeller arcs of a Vickers Viscount, about to take off from Southend Airport late in September 1974. *Big Louie* was previously named *Pont du Rhin* when it was bought by BAF on 26 March 1963, and was renamed *Plain Jane* in 1975. This aircraft first flew on 19 March 1963 and it was first registered to Aviation Traders Ltd as LX-BNG. Falcon Airways bought G-ASDC in April 1979 and reregistered it N80FA. Reregistered N103, *Plain Jane* went on to fly with Pacific Air Express and Great Southern Airways, before Yesterdays Wings Inc. bought the aircraft on 7 June 1995. *Plain Jane*'s last owner was Great Arctic Airways, which bought N103 in April 1996.
(*Paula Allen*)

TMA (Trans Mediterranean Airways) Douglas DC-6B 0D-AER in August 1974. This aircraft was accepted by North American Airlines on 15 December 1954. Trans Australia Airlines bought the aircraft as VH-TAD *John Ross* on 7 November 1963. In September 1966 this aircraft, now OD-AER, was bought by TMA. In December 1966 Echo Romeo was converted to DC-6A/B, and in December 1973, it was bought by Zantop International Airlines. LAC Colombia bought the aircraft, now HK-1707X, in April 1976. HK-1707X was lost on 8 December 1978 when it crashed at Sierra Cucuy, Bogotá, Colombia, during a cargo flight to Trinidad. (*GMS*)

Grandfatherly Warrior. Dakota 6 G-AMPZ (C-47B 44-76540) was delivered to Norwich on 7 November 1969. It was used by Rig-Air, formed to service the growing oil exploration in the North Sea, mainly to fly oil rig personnel between Holland and eastern England. When Air Anglia was founded the following year by the merger of three Norfolk-based companies – Anglian Air Charter (formed 1950), Rig-Air and Norfolk Airways (formed in 1951) – Papa Zulu became one of its first aircraft. In spring 1971 G-AMPZ was joined by a second Dakota, G-ANTD. A twice-weekly service from Norwich to Rotterdam by Dakota commenced in spring 1972. Papa Zulu was sold to Intra Airways, and departed to Exeter in February 1973 for an overhaul and respray prior to delivery to its new owners. In the 1980s the aircraft was owned by Aces High and Harvestair (Southend). Since September 1990 G-AMPZ has been operated by Air Atlantique.
(*CONAM*)

Convair 440 N4815C of Sierra Pacific Airlines at Burbank, California, in July 1974. Built as a CV-340-38, this aircraft was accepted by Delta Air Lines on 7 October 1953. It was converted to CV-440 before being withdrawn from use and stored in May 1969. It was still flying, as N153JR, as late as 1992.
(*via Barry Reeve*)

Balair Douglas DC-6A/C HB-IBS. Hunting-Clan Air Transport accepted this aircraft as G-APNO on 7 August 1958. (This company was taken over by BUA on 1 July 1970.) Balair AG bought November Oscar on 11 January 1969 and leased it to the International Red Cross during 1969 and in 1975. Balair AG kept the aircraft until September 1982, when Conair Aviation bought the DC-6, now registered C-GIBS.
(*CONAM*)

Aer Turas Douglas C-54B-1-DC EI-ADR in July 1975. This aircraft was delivered to the USAAF on 13 November 1944. It was bought by Cruzeiro do Sul as PP-CCI *Sirius* on 22 April 1946. Transocean Air Lines bought the aircraft, now N226A, on 15 June 1948. The Skymaster went on to serve with California Eastern Airlines, Air Liban and Air France, before Aer Turas bought the aircraft, now EI-AOR, on 2 June 1965. Afric

Air bought the aircraft, now ZS-IGC, on 6 November 1969. After operating with WENELA and AMAZ the aircraft, now 9Q-CAM, was bought by African Lux in August 1977. 9Q-CAM was shot down at Tete Province, Mozambique, on 26 November 1977.
(*GMS*)

LEFT AND BELOW: United States Weather DC-6A N6540C in December 1971 and September 1975. This aircraft was accepted by Trans Caribbean Airways as N6540C *Peter Johnathon* on 29 January 1958. Two years later, it was bought by the US Department of Commerce, and in September 1973 it passed to the George T. Baker Aviation School. N6540C was withdrawn from flying use and used for ground training at Miami, Florida, in September 1983. It was broken up in November 1987.
(*GMS*)

ABOVE: Martin 4-0-4 N200JS, owned by Joe Simpkins, at St Louis in February 1976. This aircraft was accepted as N40410 by TWA as '410' *Skyliner Cincinnati* on New Year's Eve 1951. Piedmont Airlines bought this aircraft on 9 March 1962, naming it *Shenandoah Pacemaker*. Finally, on 30 January 1979 the aircraft, now CP-1440, was bought by Camba Ltda. CP-1440 crashed near Apolo, Bolivia, on 14 December 1979.
(*via Barry Reeve*)

RIGHT: Southern Airways Martin 4-0-4 N253S shortly before it was sold to Marco Island Airways as N974M in November 1977. This aircraft was accepted by Eastern Air Lines on 14 April 1952 as N467A. It was then sold to Southern on 20 December 1962. It was finally withdrawn from use and stored at Billings, Montana, in February 1992.
(*via Barry Reeve*)

Zantop International Airlines Douglas DC-6B N4061K in December 1975. This aircraft was delivered to Pan Am as *Clipper Dawn* on 8 July 1953. After being bought by Aaxio Airlines on 30 June 1964, it was converted to DC-6BF in November. Several companies operated N4061K during the 1970s and Zantop leased it in April 1972, buying it outright in April 1975. In July 1990 Conifair Aviation acquired the aircraft, now C-GBYF. (*GMS*)

Music City Airways Convair 440 N4815C
in 1977. Built as a CV-340-38 it was
accepted by Delta Air Lines as '415' on 7
October 1953. Music City bought N4815C
in February 1976 and operated it for three
years. The aircraft was still flying in the
early 1990s.
(*via Barry Reeve*)

ABOVE: Naples-Provincetown Boston Airlines Martin 4-0-4 N40424 in 1979. This aircraft was accepted by TWA as *Skyliner Ohio* on 20 June 1952. Piedmont Airlines bought the aircraft on 13 July 1962 and renamed it *Pee Dee Pacemaker*. Naples-Provincetown Boston Airlines bought N4042H from Southeast Airlines on 28 November 1975.
(*via Barry Reeve*)

LEFT: Douglas DC-6B G-SIXB of Air Atlantique in 1979. This aircraft was accepted by Canadian Pacific Airlines as CF-CZV *Empress of Suva* on 15 August 1957. Zulu Victor went on to operate with Transair Sweden as *Stockholm* and Greenlandair, as *Malik*, before it was bought by Air Atlantique in March 1979. It was then operated by Air Swaziland, Interocean Airways, African Air Carriers and Transair Cargo.
(*Tony Hudson*)

RIGHT: Marco Island Airways Martin 4-0-4 N967M in 1981. This aircraft was accepted by Eastern Air Lines as N458A on 14 March 1952. After further service with East Coast Flying Service and Southern Airways, it was bought by Marco Island Airways in 1973. In June 1986 Marco Island Airways was merged with Naples-Provincetown Boston Airlines, and after being stored, N967M was sold in November 1988. In February 1993 it was bought by the City of Naples Airport Authority.
(*via Barry Reeve*)

BELOW: Convair 340-32 N14CD, still wearing its Scandinavian Beeline colours, was photographed in Florida in 1981. This aircraft was accepted by Braniff Airways on 7 August 1953 as N3428. It was then bought by Fred Olsen Flyselskap A/S on 16 September 1968 as LN-FOF. On 4 October 1976 Scandinavian Beeline bought the aircraft, now SE-GTE, and operated it for four years until it was bought by Florida Aircraft Leasing Corporation on 11 March 1980.
(*via Barry Reeve*)

Douglas DC-3 VH-MIN (42-93536) of Rebel
Air taxiing out during the October 1988 Bi-
centennial Air Show at RAAF Richmond,
near Sydney, Australia. Following RAF
service during the Second World War, this
Dakota was leased by BOAC as G-AIAZ,
and was next operated by Herald Flying
Services as VH-SNI. Rebel Air bought the
aircraft on 30 June 1983.
(*Author*)

The Skygear International Twin Pioneer passes the spectacular Sydney Harbour skyline with the Opera House in the foreground, and heads over the famous harbour bridge, on 17 October 1988. (*Author*)

LEFT: Scottish Aviation Twin Pioneer VH-EVB *Double Scotch* of Skygear International/Capricorn Air, roaring into life at Bankstown Airport near Sydney, New South Wales, on 17 October 1988. This aircraft was delivered to the Royal Malaysian Air Force on 28 May 1962 as FM1066.
(*Author*)

BELOW: Douglas DC-6BF Swingtail N867TA of Northern Air Cargo at Fort Wainwright Airport, Alaska, 4 August 1989. This aircraft was accepted by Northwest Orient Airlines on 5 October 1957 as N577. On 12 June 1964 the aircraft, now OH-KDA, was bought by Finnish carrier Kar-Air. It was converted to a Swingtail in April 1968. Trans Air Link Corporation bought the Swingtail in June 1982 as N867TA. Its next owner was Northern Air Cargo, in May 1986.
(*Author*)

Douglas DC-7C N9734Z of T&G Aviation
Inc., at Fort Wainwright Airport, Alaska, on
4 August 1989. This aircraft was accepted
by SAS as SE-CCF *Yngve Viking* on 13
December 1957. Charlie Foxtrot was badly
damaged at Khartoum, Sudan, after a
collision with an Ethiopian DC-6B, and had
to be repaired using the nose section from
N317AA. T&G Aviation Inc. leased the
aircraft in February 1977 and purchased it
outright in November 1982, operating
N317AA until BASAER Ltd bought the
aircraft, now EC-889, in July 1995.
(*Author*)

Douglas DC-3 G-AMPZ (44-76540) was built in 1945 and transferred to the RAF under the Lend-Lease scheme, operating with No. 525 Squadron at Lyneham. After two years at Silloth (1950–52), the aircraft was put into civilian service with Starways as G-AMPZ. Converted to Dakota 6 specification, G-AMPZ was later acquired by Transair and leased to West African Airways Corporation, in Nigeria. Transair then became part of British United Airlines and the aircraft was transferred to the airline's Silver City Airways subsidiary. The aircraft was then leased to various companies around the world before being bought by Air Atlantique at Coventry in September 1990. A total rebuild was completed in May 1991.
(*Author*)

Curtiss C-46A-60-CK N7768B of Rich International Airways, seen from a Chalks Grumman Mallard en route from Watson Island, Miami, to Nassau, on 29 March 1992. C-46F-1-CU N3914, operated by the Islands of Bahamas, crashed into the sea five kilometres north-west of Nassau on 2 April 1969.
(*Author*)

Douglas DC-6A/C CP-1282 of La Cumbre, at La Paz, Bolivia, where it is now used for spares, photographed on 3 November 1992. This aircraft was delivered to Loide Aereo Nacional of Brasil (later VASP) on 29 December 1958 as PP-LFD *Pernambuco*. La Cumbre bought the aircraft in 1977 and used the DC-6C as a meat hauler until it was withdrawn from service and put into store at La Paz.
(*Peter Garwood*)

Reflected Glory. Martin 4-0-4 N469A *Silver Falcon*, formerly of Eastern Air Lines, at Sun N' Fun, April 1992. Although initially used to fill in for Constellations on short- and medium-haul routes, the 4-0-4s served throughout the entire Eastern system. N469A was delivered to Eastern Air Lines on 23 April 1952 and on 17 September 1962 was sold to Southern Airways as N148S. Eventually, in 1981, *Silver Falcon* was acquired by the Mid-Atlantic Air Museum at Reading, Pennsylvania, and was fully restored to airworthy condition. (*Author*)

TAVIC Curtiss C-46F CP-1280 at Cochabamba, Bolivia, on 4 November 1992. This aircraft was delivered to the USAAF in September 1945 as 44-78746. Post-war (1948–52), it flew with All Trans Airlines, on lease, and for Flying Tiger Line, as N1801M. It went to Bolivia in 1975, being bought by SAVCO on 14 October that year as CP-1280. Trans Aereos Luwior bought the aircraft in 1983. In the early 1990s it was restored by TAVIC in a Flying Tiger Line colour scheme with TAVIC title, and used as a meat hauler. (*Peter Garwood*)

ABOVE: Servivensa Douglas DC-3C YV-610C at Kavac, near Angel Falls, Venezuela, on 8 November 1992. (*Peter Garwood*)

RIGHT: SELVA Colombia Curtiss C-46A-35-CU HK-3150 was photographed at Villavicencio, Colombia, on 12 November 1992. It has previously served in Panama and the USA, and with the Israeli Air Force. This aircraft was delivered to the USAAF as 42-3679 on 27 February 1944 and, after serving with a number of airlines, was bought by SELVA in November 1984. (*Peter Garwood*)

Rutaca Douglas DC-3C YV-218C at Kavac, near Angel Falls, Venezuela on 8 November 1992. YV-218C and YV-610C are used for tourist charters.
(*Peter Garwood*)

Trans Oriente Douglas C-53D (42-68825)
HK-2213 at Villavicencio, Colombia, on 12
November 1992. Post-war, this Dakota
operated with TWA and North East Air
Lines as NC44998, and later Lake Central,
Houston Aviation, Jefferson State Air Lines
and Air O'Hare International, before
the registration was cancelled in 1977. In
July 1979 NC44998 was impounded in
Colombia, reregistered HK-2213 and
bought by SELVA.
(*Peter Garwood*)

LEFT: Curtiss C-46F-1-CU HK-3079X at Villavicencio on 12 November 1992. This aircraft was delivered to the USAAF on 8 August 1945 as 44-78715. As B-920 N67985 it flew with Flying Tiger Line (1950) and Air Asia (1963), and it also saw service with the Colombian Air Force in 1982 as FAC 931. HK-3079 was bought by Programa Coinco in July 1994. It crashed into a hillside near Villavicencio on 9 May 1995. (*Peter Garwood*)

BELOW: Aerosol Colombia Curtiss C-46F-1-CU HK-400 at Villavicencio, on 12 November 1992. This aircraft was delivered to the USAAF in July 1945. Postwar, it operated with Riddle Airlines and Zantop Air Transport, before arriving in Colombia on 2 March 1966. HK-400 was operated by several Colombian carriers, the last of which was Aerosol. HK-400 crashed at La Colina, thirty kilometres east of Villavicencio, on 31 August 1993. (*Peter Garwood*)

RIGHT: Lineas Aeras El Dorado Douglas C-47A-DL (42-24339) HK-2666 at Villavicencio on 12 November 1992. This Dakota was issued to the RCAF in September 1943. Post-war, it served in Muscat and Oman, Norway and Canada. It was operated by Ontario Central Air Lines as C-GSTA before the registration was cancelled in September 1981, to become HK-2666 with El Dorado.
(*Peter Garwood*)

BELOW: SADELCA Douglas DC-3 (C-49J-DO 43-1962) HK-1212 taxies in at Medellín, Colombia, on 13 November 1992. This photograph cannot convey the strong aroma of coffee when the doors were opened! As NC30081, this aircraft was operated by TWA from 1944 to 1953, and by Union Steel and Beldex Corporation in 1953–54. On 28 December 1960 the aircraft received its HK-1212 registration. Cessnyca LTDA bought HK-1212 in April 1971 and after storage (1975–77), it was bought by SADELCA. HK-1212 suffered a bomb explosion on 8 February 1982, but was later returned to airworthy condition.
(*Peter Garwood*)

TRADO (Transporte Aereo Dominicano) Convair 440 HI-594CT at Santo Domingo, Dominican Republic, on 15 November 1992. This aircraft was built as a CV-340-38 and was accepted by Delta Air Lines as N4816C '416' on 7 October 1953. After conversion to CV-440, this aircraft was operated by Aspen Airways and Sierra Pacific Airlines amongst others.
(*Peter Garwood*)

Jambo! In the 1950s air services sprang up in Kenya. The best known was East African Airways Corporation (EAAC) and the majority of its airliners were converted Second World War types, such as the Douglas Dakota. EAAC was owned by Kenya, Uganda and Tanganyika (now Tanzania), with services operated between the three capital cities at Nairobi, Entebbe and Dar-es-Salaam respectively, and many towns in between. By 1955 ten Dakotas were flying EAAC routes throughout East Africa, and further afield to Salisbury, Rhodesia (now Zimbabwe), Durban, South Africa, and Zanzibar. Two of those Dakotas, C-53 (41-20120) 5Y-BGU (foreground) and C-47B-DK 5Y-AAE (behind), were still in use with Air Kenya at Wilson Airport, Nairobi, late in February 1993. Though most flights were within Kenya, charters were often flown into neighbouring Uganda and Tanzania. The twenty-five seats could be removed for freight charters. (*Author*)

C-53 5Y-BGU, shown at Wilson Airport late in February 1993, was built in 1941–42 at Santa Monica, California. During the Second World War it operated with the USAAF, and in August 1946 it was purchased by Iberia Airlines as EC-DAL. Alpha Lima was transferred to the Spanish Air Force on 9 December 1965 as a T3-58 training aircraft at Matacan AFB, Salamanca, until 18 April 1978. It then operated in the Sudan, flying cargo for the Kenana Sugar Company, before being sold to Caspair Ltd (later Sunbird Aviation Ltd). The company continued to operate the C-53 under its Sudanese registration, ST-AHK, until 1980, when it was grounded and cannibalised to keep other DC-3s flying. In November 1987 Sunbird Aviation Ltd was merged with Air Kenya (formerly Wilkenair Ltd, which had begun operation in 1966) to form Air Kenya Aviation. In January 1990, Air Kenya decided to rebuild ST-AHK and on 16 May it was registered 5Y-BGU. Golf Uniform made its first flight on 9 March 1991, and by January 1993 it had logged over 29,500 hours. (*Author*)

ABOVE: 5Y-AAE (c/n 32884), one of two C-47Bs built consecutively at the Douglas Oklahoma City factory in late 1944, was bought by EAAC on 25 February 1952. C/n 32884 was built in 1944 for the RAF as a Dakota Mk IV (KN418) and in March 1945 made regular trooping flights to India. Post-war, it was used mainly to deliver mail and newspapers to the forces stationed in Europe. In November 1947 it was assigned to No. 1 Parachute Training School at Ringway, Manchester, where it operated until July 1950. Whilst in EAAC service, KN418 became VP-KJQ *Lord Delamere*. Following independence in 1963, VP-KJQ was reregistered 5Y-AAE in August 1964.
(*Author*)

RIGHT: The second C-47B (c/n 32845/ KN419) joined the SEAC fleet on 21 June 1945. On 21 January 1949 it took part in the Berlin Airlift, and on 17 November 1950 it joined KN418, which had arrived on 26 July, in storage at Silloth, pending sale. Both aircraft were bought by EAAC, KN419 becoming VP-KJR *Sir John Kirk*. With independence, VP-KJR became 5X-AAQ, later 5Y-BBN. In 1977 5Y-BBN was sold to Caspair and used to fly tourists from Nairobi to game lodges and camps in the Mara. In 1979 Caspair was renamed Sunbird Aviation Ltd and flights now included tourists' stores and provisions as well as the passengers. 5Y-BBN was cannibalised for spares in 1992.
(*Author*)

In 1977 EAAC also sold 5Y-AAE to Caspair and it operated with Sunbird Aviation and Air Kenya Aviation. Alpha Echo is pictured, on 23 February 1993, at the rudimentary strip at Keekorok near Keekorok Lodge in the Masai Mara game reserve after a flight over the volcanic floor of the Great Rift Valley from Wilson Airport. Tourists from Keekorok Lodge Hotel prepare to board 5Y-AAE for the flight to Wilson, while a Masai tribesman is on hand to wish them *bon voyage*. 5Y-AAE and 5Y-BGU were finally retired in December 1997 and they were replaced by two Dash-7s.
(*Author*)

Douglas DC-3-314A NC25666 was purchased by Braniff Airways and delivered on 20 June 1940. It was redesignated DC-3A with Pratt & Whitney Twin Wasp engines fitted, and sold to Trans-Texas Airways in April 1953. In 1968 the aircraft was sold to Texas International and was then acquired by Tradewinds Airmotive Inc. of San Antonio, Texas, on 4 February 1969. In September 1970 the DC-3A was bought by Air Mid America Inc. Air New Zealand operated the aircraft during 1971–77. On 28 April 1977 it was purchased by Cryderman Air Service. Operated briefly by Century Airline in 1978, it was sold to Naples-Provincetown Boston Airlines on 13 June 1978 as N139PB. It was then operated by PBA and The Great Silver Fleet of Eastern Air Lines (EAL) in Naples, Florida. At its height, EAL operated over sixty DC-3s. Eastern retired its last three remaining DC-3s on 31 January 1953. With the demise of Eastern Air Lines in 1990, Starflite Corporation offered N139PB for sale in *Trade-A-Plane* in April 1991. It was purchased by Alexander Aeroplane Company on 18 July and flown to Griffin, GA, where it has been completely restored to its original condition by company employees.
(*Author*)

ABOVE: Ex-USN Douglas R4D-7 (C-47B 44-76773) SAEP (Servicios Aereos Petroleras) HK-2494 at Villavicencio, Colombia, on 10 September 1994. SAEP purchased HK-2494 on 16 September 1980.
(*Peter Garwood*)

LEFT: Aliansa Douglas C-47A (42-92071) HK-337 at Villavicencio on 10 September 1994. This Dakota operated with the 8th and 9th Air Forces during the Second World War and was bought by KLM as PH-TCM on 9 May 1946. ARCA operated HK-337 from April 1954 until it was withdrawn from use in September 1972.
(*Peter Garwood*)

RIGHT: SELVA Colombia Curtiss C-46A-35-CU (42-3679) HK-3150 at Villavicencio on 10 September 1994. This aircraft was delivered to the USAAF on 27 February 1944. Post-war, it served with several operators, including the Israeli Air Force and Seven Seas Airlines as *Baltic Sea*. Southern Air Transport bought the aircraft in August 1982, selling it to SELVA in November 1984. It was sold to an unknown operator in October 1995.
(*Peter Garwood*)

BELOW: Interandina Douglas DC-6B HK-1700 at Villavicencio on 10 September 1994. This aircraft was accepted as I-LAND by Linee Aeree Italiane on 24 July 1954, and arrived in Colombia twenty years later. It was converted to DC-6BF, registered HK-1700X, and operated by Cessnyca Colombia and Aeronorte Colombia, before Interandina bought the aircraft in 1993.
(*Peter Garwood*)

When photographed at La Paz, Bolivia, on 23 September 1994, Curtiss C-46A-5-CU CP-746 was on lease to Servicios Aereos Cochabamba from its owners TA Universal. It is reported to have smelled like an abbattoir! This C-46A, which was delivered to the USAAF as 41-12290 in February 1943, has served with various cargo carriers. From 1965, as N91295, it was operated by C-46 Parts Inc. The following year, N91295 went to Bolivia as CP-746.
(*Peter Garwood*)

SASA (Servicios Aereos Santa Ana) Convair 440 CP-2142 at La Paz, Bolivia, on 23 September 1994. Built as a CV-340-48, it was accepted by KLM as PH-TGG *Nicolaas Maes* on 16 October 1953. It served with various operators until being delivered to Bolivia in March 1987 for operation with Frigorifico Reyes. In August 1993 it joined SASA. On 22 May 1995 CP-2142 crashed while making a forced landing at San Borja, Bolivia, after an engine failure. (*Peter Garwood*)

LEFT: Frigorifico Santa Rita C-46D-10-CU CP-973 at La Paz on 23 September 1994. This aircraft was delivered to the USAAF in December 1944 as 44-77545. In March 1969 it was bought by C-46 Parts Inc., as N32227, and it was delivered to Aerovias Las Minas in Bolivia on 7 March 1972 as CP-973. Transportes Aereos Bolivar bought the aircraft in 1982, and it was next purchased by Aerovias Las Minas in 1984. It joined Frigorifico Santa Rita in 1993. (*Peter Garwood*)

BELOW: Douglas C-47B-30-DK (44-76656) CP-1419 at Cochabamba, Bolivia, on 25 September 1994. This Dakota was bought by Aerolinas La Paz in January 1981 and then acquired by Transalfa in June 1982. (*Peter Garwood*)

Air North DC-3 C-FIMA *Yukon Musher* at Whitehorse, Alaska, on 25 July 1996, when it was used to haul cargo in the 'Great White North'. Mike Alpha was originally built as 42-92847 and delivered to the USAAF on 6 March 1944. Issued to the 8th Air Force on 26 April 1944, the next day, it transferred to the 9th Air Force, where it took part in the D-Day landings, 6 June 1944. 42-92847 returned to the USA on 4 August 1945 and was sold as surplus, like thousands of Gooney Birds. It became NC88874 with United Gas Corporation and then in 1953, went to Union Producing Co., who operated this aircraft until 1967. From then on NC88874 was used by several operators, including Church of God Union Assembly, Air New England, and Air Indiana, among others. Now registered N844TH, this pure 'freight dog' has a cargo interior and built-in winch located by the cockpit that can pull freight pallets into the side doors. It is based at Chandler Memorial Airport, Arizona, and is intended for cargo service, perhaps hauling car parts from nearby Mexico.

(*Graham Dinsdale*)